Montana Montage

Montana Montage

✦

Memoir of a Dude Wrangler

Clarence Mitchell

iUniverse, Inc.
New York Lincoln Shanghai

Montana Montage
Memoir of a Dude Wrangler

iUniverse books may be ordered through booksellers or by contacting:

iUniverse
2021 Pine Lake Road, Suite 100
Lincoln, NE 68512
www.iuniverse.com
1-800-Authors (1-800-288-4677)

ISBN-13: 978-0-595-37845-6 (pbk)
ISBN-13: 978-0-595-67574-6 (cloth)
ISBN-13: 978-0-595-82219-5 (ebk)
ISBN-10: 0-595-37845-5 (pbk)
ISBN-10: 0-595-67574-3 (cloth)
ISBN-10: 0-595-82219-3 (ebk)

Printed in the United States of America

This book is dedicated to my faithful companions and drivers
who have seen to it that I am not isolated
during the final phase of my mortality:

Bill and Cathy Clark

Harlan and Judy Corrie

Donald Dusing

Dr. Lowell Edwards

Patricia Erdman

Buckshot Henderson

Everette Kested

Ada Manby

David and Sylvia Saunders

Morris (Bud) Wiener

David (Cork) Wright

and Rose Mary (Sheely) Avey, copy editor, house-
keeper, companion, and sports car driver of long
and short trips throughout the realm.

Contents

Acknowledgments

Rose Mary Avey. Faithful copy editor as the book took shape.

Eric C. Welch. Librarian, Mitchell Library, Highland Community College, Freeport, Illinois. His persistence and technological savvy helped get the manuscript to publication.

Roger and Patricia Martin. Retired University of Illinois personnel who have ordered and organized the manuscript to a professional degree.

We cleared our camps where the buffalo feed,
Unheard-of streams were our flagons;
And I sowed my sons like apple-seed
On the trail of the Western wagons.

—Stephen Vincent Benét from
The Ballad of William Sycamore
(1790–1871)

Prologue

Old men are subject to their dreams, and in my case, dreams come just before dawn. One dream keeps repeating itself, a memory from my youth—the summer I spent in Montana in 1931.

The figures stride across the stage of my mind, and the voices of the players are heard again. The towering landscape of the rimrock, the low comedy, and the tragedy all become reality again. The ghosts of that country, west of the wide Missouri, all come back to haunt me.

The dust devils, dancing sixty feet in the air, were part of the tragedy, driving the drylanders off their land that sweltering summer. The people in the trail towns and the saloons contributed a rough humor to the scene. Woven together, the land and people formed the fabric of Montana at that time.

I often awaken from my dream trembling with anticipation. Then, fully awake, I realize that it is all gone, never to return. But still, these memories are precious to me. They are my ringside seat at a panoramic cavalcade of history, the transition from the Old West to the New West.

When I was in Montana in 1931, the Old West was in transition. Many of the heroic figures that drove the big herds up the Chisholm Trail and the Goodnight Trail were alive and well: still choking on the dust of the trail, fording streams and rivers, and heading to the railheads along the Union Pacific and to Montana, where the great grass, the buffalo grass, grew.

A college professor once said that, after religion, grazing grass was probably the greatest cause of war. In fact, Genghis Khan was looking for grass when he was moving his horsemen into what we now call Europe, where the infidel was defeated. Having grass in those tribal days was a matter of survival.

It was the fortune of time and place that enabled me to meet the characters introduced in this book and to witness life on the Western frontier early in the twentieth century. For a young man from the small town of Mt. Morris, Illinois, the experience provided an adventure that has lived in my memory for an entire lifetime, a lifetime that now spans nearly a century.

Historical Introduction

Saga of the "Cousin Jacks"

In a country churchyard in Elizabeth, Illinois, stands the gravestone of my grandpa, Edward Albert Mitchell. The lead line states, "Born in County Cornwall, England."

He and other Cousin Jacks—Cornishmen—were drawn to America by the massive lead strike at Galena, Illinois. The Cornish were hard-rock miners who worked mines around the world. They built the tunnels and the massive stone walls throughout the country.

The Cornish found pick and shovel mining at the Galena strike. They were beginning to use explosives in place of backbreaking hand labor.

Grandpa moved to Elizabeth, Illinois in 1832 and shortly thereafter married Mary Sincox and started a family. But in 1850, his Cornish blood drew him to the great California gold strike, and he took passage on a wagon train out of St. Joe, Missouri.

The wagon train was ill-prepared for the perilous, five-month journey to San Francisco, and only aid from the Indians made the long trek possible. The wagon train frequently made camp at night still within sight of its starting point that morning.

When he arrived in California, Grandpa teamed up with a partner and staked a gold claim. It was not a large vein, but it was constant. For several years they hid each day's take under a rock ledge bordering a nearby stream. But one morning Grandpa awakened to find that his partner had vanished with all of the gold.

Forced to take a job to raise a new grubstake, Grandpa rode shotgun for Wells Fargo. It was, indeed, a precarious job! The average life span of a shotgun rider was only a few weeks, so Grandpa abandoned this job as soon as he had sufficient funds for another shot at mining.

At the end of twelve years, with $50,000 in gold, he was ready to go home. Disenchanted with the overland wagon journey, he decided to sail home around "The Horn." Though many ships had been lost rounding Cape Horn, Grandpa made up his mind to take the chance. He had been gone too long from home.

Landing in Philadelphia, he bought a watch, a necklace of fine web gold, and a watch charm of moss agate. Laden with his gold and those precious pieces, he took the train to Chicago and finally returned to Elizabeth, Illinois, where Grandma waited. It must have been a great homecoming. They had had six children before he left, and six more were born in the years after his return.

Grandpa's $50,000 in gold would be worth about $1 million today, but he was not a savvy investor. Friends advised him to cross the river into Iowa to buy a few thousand acres of prairie at the government price of $1.25 an acre. However, Grandpa was an adventurer, not a farmer, so he settled for a pretty piece of bottomland that backed up to a cove in the hills of Jo Daviess County. The Apple River flowed through his land.

He used his hard-rock skills to build a "dressed" limestone blockhouse home, which still stands today. Nearby, he channeled a stretch of the river into a race of fast water that turned a mill wheel.

A small settlement grew up around the mill, the focal point of the community. "All roads led to Mitchell Mill."

The mill, however, was plagued by sporadic flooding and damage to the dam. Frequently, the French millstones had to be recut by expensive experts from the city. As well, the milling industry was on the move to St. Paul and cities on the upper Mississippi.

Grandpa also helped finance a mill at Hanover. When it eventually closed, he was paid in paper money that was almost worthless.

The family spread out, and the aging couple spent the rest of their time in the stone house by the river. Grandpa died in his eighties. Grandma had gone before him.

Several generations of Mitchells are scattered around the country. However, there are only a few of us left who know the saga of the family.

Cornwall

Long after Grandpa was gone, and even many years after my Montana trip, I visited our ancestral home of County Cornwall, England. I found myself overwhelmed by the thunder of the sea crashing against the ancient cliffs, an ongoing drama that had chiseled those headlands for eons.

As I stood in the dooryard of a 700-year-old farm, a revelation swept over me: How old this land of my forefathers is, and how young Montana is, still emerging as a frontier in the American West.

How the West Was Won

The West was won by a host of larger-than-life figures who strode across the vast stage that runs from the Missouri to the Pacific. Carried on the wave of history, some were heroic—some were less than heroic.

Officially, the saga began when Thomas Jefferson, without permission from Congress, purchased this immense empire from France. Napoleon Bonaparte, who had impoverished the treasury of France, needed cash to carry on his wars in Europe. For $15 million, or about three cents an acre, Jefferson made the greatest real estate purchase in history. This acquisition included what is now the state of Montana.

The mountain men who penetrated those great expanses around the time of Lewis and Clark carried with them an epochal invention, the Kentucky long rifle. The first weapon with a rifled barrel, the long rifle propelled a bullet with unerring accuracy over great distances, depending on the eye of the rifleman. The mountain men were fur traders who intermingled and married into the Indian tribes. Their long rifles played a crucial part in the winning of the West.

Established in London in 1670, the Hudson's Bay Company dominated New World fur trading for some 200 years. The English, under General Wolfe, had conquered Quebec in 1749, and broke the French dominance of the region.

The company established a reputation among the Indians as square dealers, trading pure-wool, full-measurement blankets for the Indians' furs.

The Hudson Bay Company was headquartered in London, but its reputation and its fair-trading stores became legend throughout the Northwest Territory. Now headquartered in Toronto, Hudson's Bay Company is known today for its department stores throughout Canada.

Under a wave of American migration, inspired by the battle cry "Fifty-four-forty or fight," the Hudson's Bay Company was forced to cede the southern boundary of Canada to American mountain men and the surge of land-hungry settlers. The influx of heroic immigrants—men and women alike—played a major role in the winning of the West.

The wagon trains crawled painfully westward on their long trek from such points as St. Joe, Missouri. Their trails remain imprinted on the earth today, still visible from the airways.

Then came the cowboys and remittance men who trailed the big cowherds up the Chisholm and Goodnight Trails into the grass ranges of Montana and Wyoming. They were soon joined by the gamblers, prostitutes, gunfighters, and saloonkeepers who also played a role in the winning of the West.

Author's Note

There could be some question about the relevance of the Introduction. In its defense, I must state that it all has a distinct connection with my history. My intent is to emphasize the startling contrast between the age-old Duchy of Cornwall in England and the so-new country across the Missouri named Montana.

I also want to make note of the Cornish who helped to settle the West. With few exceptions, historians have largely ignored their great contribution.

My grandpa was known by the Cousin Jacks at Galena, Illinois; in Colorado; Alaska; and as a forty-niner in California. Somehow or other, I feel that I have paid a debt to history by speaking of the Cousin Jack Cornishmen.

Furthermore, I believe my synoptic profile of the West is relevant to my adventure in Montana. The tying together of historic footnotes is a good part of this effort.

This book could be termed something of an anthology based on personal contacts with real characters. The stories are essentially factual with some fictional coloring.

Onward to the West

I was just twenty-four years old and engaged to my sweetheart, Margaret, who was pursuing her education at the University of Michigan. When I asked her father for her hand, he objected, insisting that she continue working toward her degree. "Why can't she finish here in Mt. Morris where there is a good small college, and we could get married?" I asked him. He remained adamant, and, in retrospect, I can see that he should have kicked my butt out the door because his daughter and I came from entirely different social classes in our little town.

As though to cap his case, he said, "And how do you expect to support my daughter?" When I replied that I had $1,400 in the bank, I could see a small sparkle in his eyes. He said, "Well, maybe it will work out."

Despite this softening of his attitude, it still appeared that my marriage had been postponed, so I decided to go west for adventure before settling down as so many of my friends had. Work was slow at Kable Brothers Printing Company where I was a journeyman printer, so it was easy to arrange an indefinite leave of absence.

My juices were flowing freely. For generations the Mitchells have had an itchy foot, a restlessness that manifested itself in me as a longing to go west. I was sure that the stars foretold that my destiny was on the road west.

One bright morning in May, I set out in the 1929 six-cylinder Dodge I had bought in Rockford for $1,060. At that time a Model T Ford cost something like $400. The six-cylinder was the offspring of the famous four-cylinder Dodge, praised for its indestructible engine. It was a car that couldn't be worn out. The Dodge salesmen said it could do anything but swim a river. Unfortunately, by the time I made my purchase, the Dodge brothers had sold out, and the six-cylinder I bought was no match for its predecessor.

That was the first—and only—car I went into debt for. It was financed by an outfit in Champaign, Illinois, and I sent them a check every month. After going into debt for the Dodge and seeing my father go broke, I resolved never to go into debt again to purchase a car—and I never did.

Struck with travel fever, I did not take long to realize my dream. I found an ad in *Outdoor Recreation*, a magazine that we published at Kable Brothers, which offered a summer of excitement and adventure working on a dude ranch near Billings, Montana. The editor of the magazine, Paul Whipple, helped me respond to the ad. The position provided room and board plus $1 per day in wages. The owners of the ranch, Buford and Hazel Kratz, responded positively to my letter of inquiry, so I packed my belongings into the Dodge and headed for Montana.

As I approached the great river bridge in East Dubuque, going west into Iowa, I saw a man walking toward the bridge, his body draped with a sandwich board. The board proclaimed in large letters, "On to Montana." I thought I could use some company for the 1,400-mile trip to Billings, so I stopped and picked him up. I figured I could let him out in the next town or say that I had gone far enough if I later decided that it was a mistake to give him a ride.

In reality, Roger Thiessen, a young theologian from Wheaton College, turned out to be a good traveling companion. We became well acquainted on our long journey. Such travel requires an intimacy that can make or break a friendship. Even though I have not seen or heard from Roger since then, he left a definite mark on me.

My father was a veterinarian, a man of science, and also an atheist. With regard to religion, he did not try to influence my brother, Walter, or me, but we did have a somewhat skeptical picture of theologians. However, Roger's devotion, sincerity, and enthusiasm for Christianity certainly made an imprint on me. I think it probably played a part in my later spiritual life.

Roger's parents were Norwegian. They had gone west as drylanders who settled along a small spring. They set up their own irrigation system, allowing them to survive and to become fairly prosperous wheat farmers. Roger was going home for the harvest. He was travel wise, for this was a time when people had little money, and hitchhiking was an accepted means of travel.

The era of the hitchhiker was an age of innocence. As part of that young and relatively ingenuous society, we didn't hesitate to pick up wayside travelers. Everyone was taken at face value. College students hiked halfway across the country almost as quickly as an automobile tourist could make the trip in his own car. They were accepted without question. Today a hitchhiker would be lucky to get safely across the country. In those days it was different.

Towns were few and far between, but Roger had hitchhiked our route before and knew where to stop. Even today it is nearly one hundred miles between some towns west of the Missouri. We occasionally stopped at a YMCA where we could take a shower, swim in the pool, and stay the night for $1.25.

We sped through Iowa, down the gravel and dirt roads and through rich cornfields. We drove down the elm-shaded streets of the villages with white houses set back on well-kept lawns. As we crossed into South Dakota, the lush vegetation faded and the shade trees dwindled. Farther west the growth grew sparser, and only cottonwoods traced the watercourses. Long vistas of open land seemed to roll on forever.

Beyond the Missouri, the plains and rangelands were parched from the long drought. Grasshoppers, followed by dust storms, had laid waste to the land. It was brown and desolate. Times were hard and the living thin. The only green strips of living plants were along the streams.

Perhaps the Indians were right in believing that only grass was meant for this land. Deserted homesteads dotted the arid landscape where dryland farmers had left barren homesteads, taking only what they could carry.

As we headed west, the Dodge developed a vibration that became a shimmy whenever I exceeded forty-two miles an hour, shaking the entire car. West of the Mississippi River, nearly all the roads followed the contours of the land, scooped and graded into a roadway. Stretches of spiny rock terrain were known as washboard. Appropriately named, the washboard greatly increased the shimmy and vibration. Both preservation of the car and physical comfort limited our speed.

In contrast to the snug, sheltered valleys and fence-lined roads of northwest Illinois, there were few travelers on the road in Iowa and beyond. The tireless expanse of the West seemed endless. We became toy men in a toy car, lost in the land of sky and distance.

By strange coincidence, we ran into a trucker from Thiessen's home community. He was deadheading, running empty, back to Thiessen's home area in Montana. This was an opportunity that Roger could not ignore, so we parted company. I last saw him through a cloud of dust as the big rig disappeared over the range. I recall the empty feeling of loneliness I felt upon his departure.

Roger Thiessen has remained imprinted on my memory, and I often wonder what happened to him and whether he is still among us.

I remember stopping one late afternoon by a long, low haystack where a man was working a team of horses harnessed to a buck rake. It was some miles east of Sundance, Wyoming. As I hailed him, he stopped his team and wiped his face. "How far is it to a town where I can put up for the night?" I queried. He thought for a moment before he replied, "It's nearly fifty miles, and it'll cost you $2.50 when you get there, probably long after dark." I agreed this was a stiff price, indicating that I would probably travel for awhile, then sleep in the car.

Close to the haystack there was a windmill pumping a water well. Noting that it was a "Woodmanse" made in Freeport, Illinois, I told him I was from near Freeport and asked for a drink of water. He quickly found a tin cup. Cold water is wonderful in a dry country.

As I drank he sized me up. After I finished, he said, "I have a tarp here and a couple of old blankets. Why don't you sleep on top of the stack?" I helped him with his haying for the next hour or so, and before he left, he gave me a thick lamb sandwich from his lunch. I never slept better than I did that night—beneath the stars of Wyoming. I can still feel the softness and smell the fragrance of newly mowed alfalfa.

The next day I headed north, passed the Little Bighorn, and entered Montana. After more than a week of long days and dusty travel, I arrived at Billings.

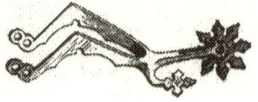

Billings

Billings was an overgrown village vying with Great Falls to be the largest city in Montana. It sat alongside the Yellowstone River, where it cut through rimrock bluffs. Entering the town, I was struck by a sculpture, a great likeness of movie star William S. Hart, which stood at a high point on the bluff. Dramatized by a spotlight, Mr. Hart is forever looking down upon the city and the river.

I went to the YMCA, got an overnight room, and had a shower. Wanting to make a good impression when I went to the ranch, I went to a tailor shop, where I took off my pants and stood in a barrel while the tailor pressed my best clothes for fifty cents. Early on, I discovered denims were the uniform for both work and dress in the West, where Levi Strauss and Company had already made their mark.

Later that day I contacted N. G. Ashley, the editor of a Western magazine, who greeted me warmly and showed me around town. It seemed that most of the tribal nations were in town that night, and, as we walked the streets, it was apparent that many of the Indians knew him well.

We stopped at several bars. In one, we ran across the author Will James, who was pretty well into his cups when we arrived. At that point in his life, he was at the pinnacle of his career. His book, *Lone Cowboy*, a copy of which still resides in my library, was the number one bestseller in the nation; it also had achieved great prominence in

Europe. To celebrate his success, Will had just purchased a large ranch in the short-grass region of Montana.

His good fortune didn't last, however, and his glory days were short-lived. He was very young and, in some ways, nearly illiterate. Although this contributed, in part, to the charm of his prose, it was inevitable that he couldn't maintain the pace over the long haul.

The vision of the cowboy, the romantic character of the Old West that Will portrayed, had great appeal in those days—an appeal remains even today.

My evening with N. G. Ashley in Billings was a great introduction to Montana and a fitting prelude to my forthcoming stay at the Reverse ⅍ Bar Ranch. I went to bed that night looking forward to what the morrow might bring.

The Reverse ⚒ Bar and Its Owners

I was up with the sun and drove the Dodge into the border country of Wyoming and Montana, where the road quite suddenly dropped into the green Stillwater Valley. The headwaters of the Stillwater River originated in the Beartooth Range, bordering Yellowstone Park, and tumbled down into Montana. There were strips of green alfalfa hugging the stream, with log ranch houses sheltered by the cottonwoods and aspens along its course. The Stillwater and Rosebud Rivers converged at the little town of Absarokee, where I was to spend the summer as cabin swamper, roustabout, and wrangler on the Reverse ⚒ Bar Dude Ranch.

The owners of the ranch, Buford and Hazel Kratz, came out to greet me. They had come to Montana at the beginning of the twentieth century, driving a team of stout horses, pulling all of their belongings in a high-wheeled wagon similar to the Conestogas that carried the settlers westward.

Starting from the Canadian River that flowed through Oklahoma, they camped every night, and Buford shot small game for their evening meals. They slept beneath the wagons, where Hazel laid out the bedrolls.

Buford was a short, wiry man with weather-worn skin. He was probably five feet seven in his high-heeled boots. He had blue eyes, rather high cheekbones, and a receding hairline, which was generally topped with his worn Stetson hat.

A nervously energetic man who could not remain motionless for any length of time, he carried a 30/30 carbine in his saddle scabbard. His marksmanship was unbelievably accurate.

Hazel had brown hair, an intelligent face, and a slender body encased in the usual Levis. She was a good all-around ranch woman and an excellent cook. She canned home-grown vegetables, wild fruits, and game. Able and efficient in coping with the hardships of the Western frontier, she was, above all, a lady of quiet dignity with a reserved but pleasant personality.

They had taken out a quarter section of land where they intended to win homestead rights. After a two-year struggle with unbroken drought, they were forced to leave the homestead and seek other means of survival. Buford found a job as a buckaroo with a big cow outfit at thirty dollars a month plus keep. The outfit took on Hazel as a cook at a wage about half of Buford's. Thus they existed for two years, saved some money, and made a down payment on the Reverse ⅍ Bar Ranch on the Stillwater River. Desperate to maintain their toehold along the river, Buford and Hazel began taking in guests. It was clear that it would be impossible to sustain the ranch on the income from their small cattle herd alone.

The dude ranch industry was in its infancy. The idea of vacationing on a working ranch was new. Initially, the Reverse ⅍ Bar was a struggling ranch with only a straggle of weekend guests. A few came from Billings for short stays. Except for this meager income, the owners' immediate living had to come from the land, river, and forest. Their cash was hoarded for emergencies and necessities.

Every night they caught trout as quickly as possible for the next morning's breakfast. For me, fried trout with potatoes and homemade bread became less than the gourmet treat it would be considered today.

Even though the country was in the depths of the Great Depression, we ate well, albeit somewhat monotonously. Hazel was resourceful with what she had available and could more than make do. She canned many quarts of venison, elk, antelope, and even bear to carry the family through tough times.

There was a small flock of chickens that lived mostly on grasshoppers; however, chicken was considered a treat to be reserved for guests. Beef from the small herd was carefully held for market. A good steer could bring a nickel a pound on the hoof. Older cows (cutters and canners) went for three to three-and-a-half cents a pound. They could be turned into ready cash so they were not considered for home food supply.

When a few range cows freshened (let down their milk after calving), they were securely hobbled and milked under duress—painful for the cows and difficult for the milkers. These were not dairy cows. The milk went through a hand-turned separator, and the cream was carefully accumulated for the few dollars it would bring in town. The skim milk was used at home. This was long before skim milk became the vogue to trim the waistline of an affluent and sedentary society.

A lucky piece of publicity, run as filler by a benevolent editor in a national magazine, gave a boost to the growing dude ranch industry. The Burlington and Northern Pacific Railroads were beginning to publish releases from the Dude Ranches Association, which had recently organized in Sheridan, Wyoming.

The Eaton Ranch was one of Wyoming's first recognized dude ranches. It won fame as the setting of a multitude of romantic Western books.

By a historical coincidence, I later became the production editor of one of the earliest publications of the industry. I wrote the romance copy and laid out the formats for a six-by-nine-inch, thirty-two-page booklet.

The dude ranch was an innovation that carried a strong appeal for people searching for the excitement and adventure of the West. The word *dude* was a generic term used by the natives of the West to identify people from the East. *Dude* eventually came to be considered a derogatory term by a sophisticated ad agency, inspiring the not-so-subtle change to "guest."

Reverse OR Kratzir Ranch, and Indian Signal Point Absaroka, Mont.

Reverse ⅍ Bar Ranch

Gradually, things were beginning to look up at the Reverse ⅋ Bar Ranch on the Stillwater. A few guests were appearing from outside Montana, some from as far away as Chicago. The out-of-staters always stayed longer, and they spent more money. More log cabins were built along the river to accommodate the growing number of guests at the Reverse ⅋ Bar.

When I first arrived at the ranch, however, Buford and Hazel were still struggling to stay afloat. Buford eventually raised my $1 a day pay to $1.25, but he and I both knew I would never get it. He didn't have the $1.25.

The Big Decision

Buford's parents had settled in Billings before Buford and Hazel and over a period of years had established a thriving dairy farm on the edge of the community. Milk distribution from the outside had not appreciably penetrated the West, and dairy products were scarce.

Shortly after I arrived at the Kratz ranch, I noticed that there was considerable conversation—followed by periods of silence—concerning a proposition offered by Buford's father.

Ready to retire, Buford's father had offered the younger couple the opportunity of a lifetime. Buford and Hazel were to move to town to take over the dairy operation, which offered the certainty of a regular income. This could be a turning point! It offered Buford and Hazel an opportunity to escape the vagaries of the cattle industry. However, it posed a major lifestyle change. Both of them were wedded to the life of the river and the far-reaching range land. Buford and Hazel had been debating the pros and cons of this change in their lifestyle for several weeks. Now the time had come to accept or reject the elder Kratz's offer.

I clearly remember that late afternoon when Buford cranked up the Chandler, and we headed for Billings. Hazel was ready to accept, but she did not want to push Buford into another way of life. Little was said during the doleful trip to town.

They both knew the time of final decision had arrived. As we neared town, Buford exploded in a final protest, "I don't want to be a damn dairy drudge hooked to a dairy farm sixteen hours a day! I will take the gamble of cattle ranching along the river and the range out on the benches rather than be a prisoner to a bunch of dairy cows." So the decision was made. They chose a life of risk and adventure. Buford's father was obviously disappointed, but he did not try to change the lifestyle of his son.

Late that night we returned to the Reverse ⅋ Bar Ranch with the moonlight dancing along the torrent of the river. Their outlook had changed, and Buford and Hazel were jovial as they pulled up to the ranch house. The die was cast, and the mood of indecision had evaporated.

Buford never lost faith in the destiny of the ranch and the river. He would often say, "Duke, there is just so much frontage along the river. It will only increase in value, and sooner or later there will be lots of buyers. The frontage will be valued at a great premium. This land and river are bound to be discovered by the boom of outlanders."

The Guests

During the summer of 1931, a rather cosmopolitan group of guests appeared at the Reverse ⅋ Bar. The visitors ranged from the local weekenders, who came mainly from Billings and the surrounding territory, to socialites from the Midwest and the East.

One of my favorite guests was Mrs. Grayson, a prominent social matron. She and her husband led separate careers. He was devoted to his profession, and she was an activist in many civic crusades. An early advocate of the conservation of Montana's pristine waters, she had a long-range view of the environment at a time when there were more people in the city of Milwaukee than in the whole state of Montana.

Mrs. Grayson rode with an English saddle pad and wore formal riding attire: a fox-hunting hat, high riding boots with spurs, hunting jacket, and pants. She was a charming extrovert and a gracious hostess at the high teas served daily in her cabin.

Agnes Rawlins was a complete contrast; her riding style and attire were entirely Western. She wore Levis, high-heeled Western boots, and Spanish-style spurs. Topped off by a Stetson hat, her rigging was all Western, and she was an expert horsewoman. Many times I saw her cut out a horse or a renegade steer with the professional skill of a buckaroo.

Agnes was the daughter of an "old" ranch family, the first of her generation to receive a degree at the University of Montana. She began her career as a legal secretary in a prominent law office in Billings. She was ahead of her time as a career woman and served as an excellent model for the young women who would follow her in the modern West.

Then there was Madam Parson. She was, literally, a madam in Billings' best house of prostitution. She did not talk shop, but she was known to all and accepted as a social and business equal by the others who sat at the table at the Reverse ⅍ Bar Ranch. On occasion, she told me, "Duke, when you are in town, stop off at my house. I will see that you get treated royally. My girls are the best and are on constant medical inspection." I never accepted her invitation, but sometimes, rather ruefully, I regret that I missed that experience.

Another visiting dude was a sophisticated, retired Boston lawyer, complete with a Harvard degree and a strong accent. This interlude in the West provided him with a taste of the adventure that he had missed during his youth. Keeping largely to himself, he smoked good cigars and drank Canadian whiskey. He also did a lot of reading and a bit of amateur fly casting under Buford's instruction One time during a visit in his cabin, he informed me that all American law was founded on the basis of the English Anglo-Saxon law, dating from the confrontation of the barons with King John. This was based on the Magna Charta, a copy of which hangs in my living room in Mt. Morris.

Janice Hudson was a tragic figure. She was a beautiful woman who suffered the traumatic break-up of her marriage. Her tragedy occurred during a wild prohibition-era party where all present had imbibed too much corn whiskey. Her husband had found her semi-conscious in the arms of another man. He sued for a quick divorce and never forgave her for that one reckless moment. She never got over him and tried to heal the wound by using alcohol as a cloak of forgetfulness. Her one mournful song was the constant refrain of *Who's Sorry Now.* She lived in a world haunted by nightmares. I never saw her after she left the ranch.

There was a Jewish lady who came from New York. She had plenty of money and stayed for over a month. Buford later said that she and a young Eastern college grad made a turning point in the fortunes of the ranch. The college grad was a scion of an old Boston family who did the usual things typical of such lineage. He went to prep school when many Easterners believed that "culture" went only as far west as Amherst. Upon graduation from an Ivy League college, he was scheduled to take the usual month's tour to imbibe the history and culture of Europe. But he had been intrigued, as were many others, with the colorful stories of the vast empire west of the Missouri, and so he became one of the guests at the Reverse ⅍ Bar that summer. Through my friendship with a road kid printer, a dropout from the Eastern school, I had procured this grad's name. Impulsively, I had written him a letter embellishing the color and country of the Reverse ⅍ Bar Ranch and itemizing the rates and program of a month's stay. Surprisingly, he responded quickly and sent a check for his reservation as a guest. The Jewish lady and the young Bostonian with the Back Bay accent were two of Buford's prized guests. He devoted so much attention to them that Hazel became a bit upset. They were both long-term guests, and, as I recall, they paid $80 a week and received the full package in Buford's dude program. This included a five-day pack trip into the Beartooth wilderness area. They followed the trail up to Lake Abundance, the source of the Stillwater River.

The care and maintenance of the guests nearly required a full-time effort by the limited hands at the ranch. I remember Buford struggling to load the packsaddles for his many pack trips with the guests. The sawbuck-shaped packsaddles were placed on the back of the docile packhorses. Buford had to load the saddles compactly and throw a diamond hitch to secure them. Throwing a diamond hitch was a graduate skill of the Western man and packer. One minor slip of the rope and the entire cargo could be lost on a mountain trail.

Horse Train in Winter

Before loading the guests' gear on the packsaddles, Buford demanded that they return their hard-sided suitcases to their quarters and repack soft packs wrapped in their slickers. These elite clients were well worth the problems they created, but they were a constant irritant to the hardworking Hazel, who had to serve their needs and whimsies at the ranch table and elsewhere. Hazel shared with Buford every step on the ladder of their success. In her quiet manner, she more than acted as the gracious hostess to their guests. She did a lot of "heavy lifting" in the daily routine of unending chores required to maintain a good establishment. Compared to the modern appliances of today, her equipment was primitive. Her manual washing machine was not much more sophisticated than a washboard. On several occasions, I was dispatched to the few remaining wheat farms out on the benches to find workers to assist Hazel with her heavy work. Unfortunately, every single worker would leave by the end of the first week, usually of his own accord. They were fully competent in performing field work but had little know-how when it came to domestic work on a dude ranch. I was pressed into service to run the washing machine. This required strong arms to pull the lever back and forth. This was no electric machine. By the time I had run through eight or ten loads, my arm was numb and practically paralyzed. I was glad, however, to relieve Hazel of a heavy chore. Buford spent a great deal of time entertaining the guests with his colorful cowboy stories, enhanced by his performances with Socks, his top cutting horse. Buford was a great storyteller. His audiences were enchanted by his tales, which helped fulfill their fantasies of the Wild West.

Through the years, Hazel and Buford each played a significant role in their long and laborious trip to success. Buford probably enjoyed their success more than Hazel, but she played the old-fashioned woman's role of being relatively unsung and unheard in their march to prosperity. They acquired myriad friends from among the many guests who came to visit and savor the experience they offered on the banks of the Stillwater.

The Rivers

To those of us who have spent most of our lives in the lush Midwest, it is difficult to conceive of the great importance of Western rivers. Water is the lifeblood of the vast region west of the Missouri. The Rosebud, Stillwater, Boulder, and their tributary streams lace the area of south-central Montana.

The rivers tumble down out of the border country of Wyoming and Yellowstone Park. The towering peaks of the Yellowstone and Absaroka Ranges, including the Beartooth Range, mark the headwaters of these rivers. The amount of snowfall largely determines the volume of water in the channels. Green strips of irrigated meadows form a contrast to the dry bench country that spreads out from the streams. This contrast of green and gray-brown is vivid to the eyes of the traveler.

The land values in the West were predicated upon the proportions of irrigated meadows to the dry-land range. Buford's spread, during the depressed thirties, was worth some two to three dollars an acre for the dry range and twenty to thirty dollars an acre for irrigated alfalfa fields. The percentage of these irrigated acreages, the feed source for the herd during the long winters, largely determined the land's carrying capacity for a beef herd. A stand of irrigated alfalfa was often good for ten years in the arid country.

Stretches of the rivers were swift, with roaring white water surging through the ranch land. The little room to which I had been assigned during my stay in Montana at the Reverse ⅋ Bar Ranch was cut into a high bank along the Stillwater. More than once I awoke in panic to the sound of the rushing river. This particular river, coursing down through the meadow, seemed to be roaring right through my bedroom. It took considerable time for me to become attuned to the rush and roar of the Stillwater.

Kratz Ranch House on the Stillwater River

There were only a few placid stretches of water in the Stillwater as it flowed through on its way to the Yellowstone. Its pristine water was the source of drinking water for the people and animals that lived along its banks. One would naturally scoop up a canteen of water to quench his or her thirst or gulp it while lying along the stream. I also found that a can of tomatoes submerged in the snow-cold water provided a wonderful respite during a hot day of hay making.

The fortunes of the ranch rested on the harvest of the hay crop. Hay harvest, fall and spring round up, and branding were busy, busy times for cattle ranchers—vital to the success of every spread.

The Stillwater Road, between Absarokee and the Kratz ranch at the foot of the Beartooth Range, rises so abruptly that the change in altitude shortens the growing season. This sudden increase in elevation in a valley is known locally as grade. The alfalfa growing season at the upper levels is a week or more shorter than in the valley. This change frequently meant the loss of the final cutting of hay in the highest fields.

There is little or no market for alfalfa in our lush Illinois countryside. In the arid areas of the West, it brings a good price and rarely seems too plentiful.

Today, Montana is a haven for many affluent Hollywood people and captains of industry who have bought large ranches in the Big Sky Country of the Treasure State. Now many of the river courses are lined with dwellings. Their waters are no longer as pure as they once were. Civilization continues to move in, and the only vestiges of the Old West remain in the isolated corners of Montana and Wyoming.

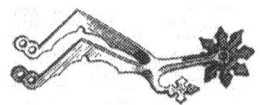

Fly Fishing

Fly casting is a classic form of fishing, which elite fisherman have enjoyed for centuries. Izaac Walton was among the great who wrote and published a reference book respected by the aficionados of the sport. His tombstone covers his remains and lies between those of the royalty buried beneath the floor of the great Winchester Cathedral in England.

His writings have carried through the years as a reference for fly casters everywhere. I am not competent to write about the grace and technique of fly casting, but in short the caster whips the line backward just enough to avoid backlash at the end before he snaps the long line forward into a graceful loop, dropping the lure lightly on the target area of the stream. This light landing on the surface creates the illusion of a live insect landing. The moment the trout strikes the artificial fly, the caster sets the hook ever so gently and firmly—so as not to tear the flesh—and works the fish back to add to his creel. Such is my oversimplification of the fly-caster's art.

The snowmelt of the lively mountain rivers of Montana are extremely cold, just the right temperature to support large numbers of trout. Each night, on a swinging bridge spanning the Stillwater River, we took turns fly casting for the next morning's breakfast. We favored the royal coachman or a brown hackle as bait. Grasshoppers were such a surefire bait that they were not considered sporting by true fly fisherman.

The majority of our Midwestern streams are too warm for trout propagation; however, the pristine waters in Montana were alive with rainbow, Lock Leven, and in the higher altitudes, cutthroat trout. I have seen Buford make a cast with two leaders on one line and come up with a trout on both.

Unlike the Midwestern corn farmer, the rancher of those days had some free-and-easy time, intervals in which he could hunt and fish, or go on visiting trips under the pretense of fence building. Ranching was a free-swinging lifestyle compared to that of the Midwestern farmer. Of course, these periods of recreation were interspersed by periods of crisis caused by the uncontrollable forces of nature.

One time we made a fishing junket through Yellowstone down into Jackson Hole, Wyoming. We were traveling very lightly. We carried only a blanket bedroll, a slab of bacon, potatoes, bread, and our fishing rods. We had very little money, and we slept under the stars.

Natural scavengers, bears often raided the garbage barrels at Yellowstone campsites. These containers were suspended on stilt-like structures four to five feet above the ground. They were designed to prevent the bears from upsetting the garbage. One night I awakened to see a bear clinging to the structure above me. Thereafter, I selected a different location for my bedroll.

Early one evening we were witness to one of the great spectacles of Yellowstone Park, when the great grizzly sloth came in to feed behind the strong fences. Several mounted rangers with loaded 30/30 rifles added to the drama of the scene. Now, most of the grizzlies are gone from Montana.

Grizzlies are the most powerful four-footed creatures on the continent. That summer a trapper was disemboweled by one stroke of a grizzly caught in a steel trap. He had mistakenly assumed that the bear had died from his rifle shot. On one occasion when Buford and I were working cattle, we came across a freshly killed steer that had been dispatched by one powerful blow from a hungry grizzly bear.

We lived quite well off the trout we caught while camping in Yellowstone Park. Trout fried with bacon, a slice of bread, and potatoes made a great meal. We lived from our fishing resources and a few chocolate bars.

The Fire Hole River ran adjacent to the boiling geyser basin in Yellowstone. There were points where a fisherman could swing a freshly caught trout into a geyser, which would cook it in a few moments. Seeing the wonders of Yellowstone, the nation's first national park, should be on the agenda of every American.

While at the ranch, I was privileged to witness one of the great fly-casting exhibitions of all time. The antagonists in this ongoing battle for supremacy were Buford and a certain Captain Grey.

Captain Grey was a West Pointer in the regular Army who commanded a National Guard company in Billings. His regiment's history dated back to Crazy Horse's victory at the Battle of Little Bighorn—Custer's last stand.

Captain Grey became a deeply devoted fly fisherman after arriving in Montana. His passion for fly-fishing made him a single-topic bore among his social contacts, so much so that his fellow guests at the Reverse ⚔ Bar Ranch were prone to sidestep his company. He approached fly-fishing as if it were a creative art form. His casting was honed to textbook perfection. The year that he was awarded

State Champion Fly Caster of Montana, his enthusiasm for fly casting eclipsed all other interests.

On various occasions, Buford, the old competitor, could not resist calling out Captain Grey for a fly-casting duel. The captain typically waded into the river, gracefully casting a royal coachman fly thirty to forty feet, usually landing near his target in the pooling water.

Buford Fly-fishing, Mounted on Socks

Mounted on his horse, Socks, Buford then rode into the thunderous current, and with his unorthodox black-snake technique, hit his target in the pool with an uncanny accuracy—far beyond that of Captain Grey.

The Captain was not very gracious in accepting his obvious defeat. He insisted that the black-snake style of casting was neither orthodox nor fair in competition. Still, he was unable to convince the observers that Buford's results were not superior to his own.

It should be noted for the record that, when all was said and done, Captain Grey remained the official Champion Fly Caster of Montana, a fact that he never let anyone forget. However, in my mind, Buford was a tad better with a fly rod.

Buford

To put it somewhat kindly, Buford was inclined to be an exhibitionist. Some of his critics would say bluntly that he was a braggart.

Buford was well-known to the Indians who lived on the reservation outside of Billings. They had their own name for every white man with whom they had contact, and once a name was chosen, it stuck and became a part of the language of the tribe.

I had noticed, whenever we were in Billings, that individual Indians always returned Buford's greeting with a name that escaped me. I couldn't quite make it out. When I asked Buford what they said, he was vague, "It was just an old nickname." One day I mentioned this to N. G. Ashley, the editor who had squired me around Billings on my first evening there and who personally knew many Indians who lived on the reservation. Ashley slapped his knee and laughed so heartily that he had to pause before answering. "Duke, you listen carefully next time, and you'll hear his Indian name. It's 'Wind-in-the-Britches.'" Then he added, "To be honest, Indians have named many white men around here with a lot worse names than that."

To some, the most exasperating part of Buford's bravado was the fact that he could always make good on his claims regarding horsemanship, marksmanship, and other activities in which he styled himself to be an expert. He was confident enough of his abilities that he rarely passed up a wager involving his acquired skills. One gentleman echoed the consternation of many others when he said that it was maddening to see Buford line up two distant magpies in his sights and kill both with one shot from his 30/30. He fired from the saddle while Socks stood as rigid as a statue under the bark of the rifle. Buford picked up the man's bet before he departed. That famous shot exemplified his many exploits that became legend in his hometown.

Early one morning Buford and I had pulled up our horses for a breather, and I took this opportunity to roll a Bull Durham cigarette. I was a bit clumsy, which prompted Buford to lean over, saying, "Pass me the makings, and I will show you how to build one of those things." Holding the strings of the bag in his teeth, he deftly rolled a solid cigarette with one hand. "There! That's the way those fake cowboys in the movies try to do it."

From a nickel sack of Bull Durham, one could make about twenty to thirty smokes. Sometimes a cowboy would wet the end of a cigarette after a few puffs and paste it to the wall above his bunk for later use.

On another occasion Buford came at me with this: "Duke, the old tongue from the hay rake broke on me today during the start of my first cutting. I'll get you up before daylight, and you can help me with the new pole tongue."

At dawn the next day Buford called for me at breakfast. I discovered he was a provident and knowledgeable man who had taken precautions a couple of years before for just this emergency. In the shed next to the corral, Buford had stored and cured several long, straight lodge-pole pine trunks. He stripped the bark and very carefully cut one pole to the proper length for a hay rake tongue. He shaved and fitted it for insertion into the buck rake. He then worked out the old broken stub, and we put the new tongue in place.

Buford loved his car, and, as we were washing it one afternoon beside the river, I asked him, "How come all the autos in this area are Chandlers of the same model year?" He replied, "Well, there was a fellow named Watkins in Columbus. He was a fine guy and a great salesman. He sold Chandlers clear up and down the Stillwater and over into the Rosebud country. As you've noticed, they're all the same model, exactly seven years old. Does that tell you something? That was the last real good cattle market. Nothing's been worth anything since."

Buford took me riding up on the benches to check on a few yearlings foraging the dry land. He said the pickings were so thin that the cows lost any gain traveling between the sparse grass and water. The dust devils were spiraling high in the air, blown from the parched abandoned wheat fields.

As we topped out on a ridge, I saw an apparition—a single file of some twelve or fourteen phantom horses floating against the skyline. As we grew closer, they showed no signs of awareness. A moving cavalcade of skeletons, they passed slowly, travelers without a destination.

We moved closer. Buford stopped, pulled his old Stetson lower and reached for the ever-present 30/30 carbine in his saddle scabbard. Then he looked closely at one of the horses nearest to him and paused. "I should do them the favor of shooting all of them, but they carry the brand of the Crow Nation," he said. "The law is hard on a white man shooting Indian horses. These poor horses will just keep on dying from eating locoweed. It's the poisonous weed that grows when the grass is burned out. They are certainly in the last stages of loco." I can still see those ghostly horses moving slowly, skylined along the ridge, traveling to their final destiny.

Montana was rattlesnake country. The drought that summer had forced the rattlesnakes to migrate down off the benches toward the watercourses. I remember one dude was struck by a rattler sunning at the edge of the river. Fortunately, he was wearing high English riding boots that saved him when the snake struck. No doubt he carried the mental scar long in his memory.

For the most part, the locals were rather casual when it came to rattlesnakes; however, there was one encounter when Buford, the old buckaroo, almost lost his cool. He had just stepped onto the porch of the ranch house when a big rattler slipped between some latticework. Buford abruptly jumped through a side door to his saddle room and emerged just as suddenly with a shotgun. There was a roar as he shot at close quarters into the wide partition where the snake had disappeared. The charge from the twelve-gauge blew out a good section of the thin wall; smoke and powder filled the porch. Then Buford let go with the other barrel. He dropped down on his knees and prodded beneath the floor with a long stick. In a short time, he scraped out a section of rattlesnake remains. With a great sigh he sat down, shaken but greatly relieved. As he looked at the shattered siding, he said, "It's a lot better to ruin a strip of partition than to tear down the entire house. I would never have been able to sleep again knowing that rattler could be anywhere in the house."

Buford had the knowledge and ability to manage nearly all the problems that surfaced at the ranch without calling on outside help. When something went wrong his first thought was how to fix it, not where to go to get help or who to call for assistance. He was a self-sufficient man with all the skills required to operate the ranch in an efficient and orderly fashion. I like to think of him as a true product of the Old West.

Buford on the Ranch

Among Buford's other good traits were his resiliency, his marvelous sense of humor, and his ability to tell a good story. He set the tone at the ranch, and his guests loved him. He was the perfect host who kept the dudes returning for more of the Western experience.

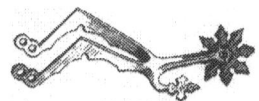

Bronc Breaking

A fully trained cutting horse like Socks, Buford's most prized possession, was a thing of beauty and utility. However, it took hours of work to bring a raw colt to the sophisticated level of a working cow horse.

The working western saddle and the western horse were inherited from the Spaniards, who, under Hernando Cortés, conquered Mexico in 1510 with 300 men on horseback. The descendants of their horses drifted northward and continue to roam the ranges of the West today.

To protect grazing rights of the cattleman, many of the wild horses were captured. Wild horse roundups were financed by the federal government. The Cattlemen's Association had a powerful lobby that promoted real and imaginary protection for the ranchers. It became a cliché that the Cattlemen's Association, Anaconda Copper, and Montana Power ran the state of Montana.

Some of the wild horses that were captured were sold off to dog food processors in Illinois and points east. Others were selected to become possible saddle horses. However, before such horses could be trained for pleasure riding or for work, they had to be rough broken or "topped off," a wild and woolly process that usually took no more than several hours.

The topping off process, or bronc breaking, was an activity found largely in the West. The trained masters of equitation in England and other countries would literally take weeks to reach the point of saddling. They would start slowly by introducing a yearling to halter leading to overcome the colt's timidity to human contact. Then they would get him to become accustomed to the gentle snaffle bit. Next would come putting on and taking off the saddle blanket and saddle. Finally, the horse would be mounted and gently urged to work by signals to the bridle.

In the West, owners of wild horses often took their horses that they considered to be too rough, or too green, or too risky to break themselves to a professional bronc fighter, a man willing to risk life and limb to tame a horse in short order for a few dollars. The old bronc fighter that I met in 1931 was bent and crippled from the many rough rides he endured while plying his trade. In his younger years he had been a champion on the rodeo circuit. He had set up shop as a blacksmith and bronc breaker at the edge of Absarokee. He also served as a farrier to balance his time and income. Even then his clientele was limited because many of the big cattle outfits carried their own horseshoer.

Once a western horse was topped off, it was ready for the rest of its training which could proceed fairly rapidly now that the horse would tolerate man and saddle on its back and a bridle and bit. The westerner taught his three-gaited horse to neck-rein by slight signals on either side of the neck. Neck-reining was essential in using the horse to work cattle on the range and in the stockyard. Five-gaited dressage was only for style in the show ring and was not a major factor in the early West.

One of the very rare occasions when Buford failed to live up to his boasting surfaced at an early-morning episode in the corral. He was going to top off an unbroken, three-year-old, ungelded colt. The colt had been neglected and had spent most of his three years on a far bit of range. He had been discovered near home quarters and was hazed into the corral the night before. Buford had gone out and looked him over and decided the colt should not go unbroken, for as the colt grew older, he might become a renegade, worthless horse.

Buford was up early the next day, and over our morning coffee, he said to me, "Delbert tried to top off this bronc and reports that he was thrown twice and then couldn't mount the saddle. So, Duke, if you want to see how a western man sets a saddle and tops off a rough one, come out to the corral."

After our usual breakfast, we walked to the corral where the young stallion had been kept for the night. When we went through the gate, the horse immediately started on a dead gallop around the corral, emitting a large squeal as he circled us. Finally, he settled for a moment and as Buford approached cautiously, he slipped a halter over the horse's neck and slipped a rope through the ring. Then he said, "Duke, come out here and pull this bronc into the snubbing post." The snubbing post was a sturdy hardwood post several inches in diameter that had been set several feet into the ground in the center of the corral.

The rope was wrapped around the snubbing post, and I proceeded to pull and tug the colt toward it. I kept pulling. The colt was struggling and squealing, resisting all the way to the post. Finally the bronc was snubbed up to the post. Buford then came to the horse, petted him, and talked to him in soothing tones. The horse pawed the ground. His nostrils showed red. He was not to be tamed.

Buford had carried the rigging, his breaking saddle, and his high-port breaking bit to the place of action. While I snubbed the horse tightly, Buford flung the blanket and saddle on the colt's back. When the saddle was in position, Buford pulled and cinched the girth. Next he humped the horse with his knee to squeeze the wind out of him while he tightened the girth further. Buford told me to hold him tightly. "Snub him as close as you can." While I held the horse, Buford, in one motion, vaulted into the breaking saddle. When I let go of the rope, immediately the bronc crow-hopped, bucked, and sundanced in the air. All four feet were off the ground. At that point, Buford was thrown from the saddle and landed on his back on the hard earth. The horse went racing, snorting, and squealing around the corral. He continued bucking until he broke the saddle loose. Buford slowly and painfully got up, brushed his back, loosened his batwinged chaps and limped back to the house without saying a word. That was one of the rare occasions when Buford didn't live up to his rhetoric. However, that horse was not typical. He was a renegade outlaw.

At that juncture my admiration for the bronc fighter grew immensely. I also decided that bronc breaking was one ranch activity that I personally would try to avoid in the future. It seemed excessive in view of my pay of $1 a day.

Midnight Canyon

Dressed in leather bat-winged chaps, I often mounted up to take the guests on short horseback trips. One outing took us through Midnight Canyon, a narrow trail where the sun reached only at brief intervals. One day in the canyon we were strung out single file, eight or ten riders with me leading the column. Buford had failed to tell me that rattlesnakes probably were lying on the ledges just overhead, catching the few rays of sun. He also forgot to mention that the rattlers were blinded by their shedding skins at this time of year and would strike at any approaching sound.

Midnight Canyon

We were well into the canyon when the horses smelled and heard the rattlers. Suddenly, they reared and plunged. We all desperately pulled leather. Horses and riders became a churning mass, twisting and turning to escape the canyon. The line had broken into bedlam. At the height of the pandemonium, Agnes Rawlins, a young woman from a local ranch, spurred her horse through the chaos. She grabbed bridles and pressed the horses to turn with such assurance that the riders and horses recovered some equilibrium. Thanks to her, we emerged with shaken nerves but no casualties.

When I thanked Agnes, I admitted that, despite my chaps and hat, I was no professional. She knew my outfit was one of Buford's props for staging the romance of the West to the dudes. "Duke, I knew you weren't a Western man. I could tell by the way you forked your horse."

Later that night, we were sipping a sample of home brew in her cabin when an incident occurred that remains clear in my memory. A mouse ran across our feet. Much to my astonishment, Agnes went into a spasm of hysteria. I shook her by the shoulders and slapped her face to bring her to her senses. When she was calm again, I expressed my surprise at her reaction.

"Agnes, it beats the hell out of me why a fine horsewoman like you had the courage and skill to break up a near catastrophe in the close quarters of Midnight Canyon and is now scared by a little mouse running along the floor." Her only reply was, "My mother told me that a mouse was a sign of evil and bad fortune at the time of my birth." I found it hard to challenge her response.

The Poker Game

Despite the hard times there was a more-or-less continuous poker game going on in Absarokee. I remember a number of evenings spent sitting beside the players.

Paper money was disdained west of the Missouri. In those days silver was regarded as the real money. The bank and the big gambling houses in Billings were lined with stacks of silver dollars.

Money was scarce in those early days of the Depression, and the ranchers frequently bet cattle instead of cash. Intervals of silence and study were broken by "Open on an early calf," followed by a call, or "Raised to a long yearling." Then, "Call or I will raise to a steer," and "Cards to the gamblers," on into the night. Finally, "I will have a look at your cards."

The nearest neighbor upstream gambled away most of his herd that summer, while a rancher downstream won enough beef to lay the foundation for a future herd.

One night as my interlude in Montana was closing, I entered the game when money was the main stake. One wrangler was reinvesting his winnings of earlier in the evening. I played my cards with a certain desperation.

My money had dwindled to just a few dollars. I was at a critical point where I either had to wire home or take a last desperate shot at the poker game. My fortunes were in the balance.

I did not need to bluff; each of my hands portrayed good fortune. Along toward morning, I sat with a full house, kings over jacks. I kept raising, and my opponent kept pace with me. After he made his final call, I laid down my hand and raked in the pot.

When Buford and I rode home, a late moon was sparkling on the river. I was carrying seventy-seven silver dollars in a canvas bag—home free with ample funds for grub and gasoline for my journey back to Illinois. This was one time when fortune did not fail me in my time of need.

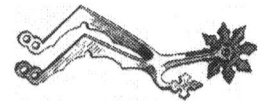

Monarch

One day Buford and I were riding up on the benches that rose from the Stillwater to the foot of the Beartooth Range. We were trying to round up Monarch, the bull, who could smell a cow in heat for miles. He had broken loose from his corral and was on a rampage. It wasn't the first time Monarch had caused Buford trouble by breeding other men's cattle.

That morning the phone rang off the wall with the cries of the upriver ranchers. "Buford, come and get your damn bull! He's running close to my cowherd. Come and get him before we shoot him and serve him up as bologna." A rampaging bull invading the bloodlines of another herd was a major crime, almost tantamount to cattle rustling on the Western range.

It was a lovely morning with a lone cloud circling the awesome peaks to the west. A solid silver streak ran down the mountainside in the distance. I said to Buford, "It's late for a snow gully even at this altitude." "That's no snow slide," Buford replied. "It's a waterfall that appears motionless in the sun."

The Beartooth dominated that piece of borderland. Its peaks provided a forever brooding and changing mood over the landscape. The only access to the interior of the mountain range was the Stillwater River trail, which led up and up into the realm of the legendary King of the Golden River. Transportation was by saddle horse and pack train only.

Buford and I rode on into the mountains and found Monarch in an upper meadow, about to engage his talents with another herd of cows. Buford spurred his horse and cut out Monarch from the herd with his black snake.

The black snake was a long leather whip with a rawhide stringer, tipped with a lead stinger. It was a formidable force when wielded by an expert, and Buford was an artist with the black snake. He could flick a cigarette out of a man's mouth at twenty feet.

Monarch was reluctant to be turned away from his pursuit, but Buford cut him out of the herd and headed him toward home. He snapped the black snake and bellowed, "Get home, you dirty bastard. You can't breed any more of these cattle and get me in any more trouble."

Monarch would run for a short distance, then look back at Buford with a benign expression. Buford would shout, "Get moving you son of a biscuit." Then he would punctuate the statement with a snap of the black snake over Monarch's nose. And so it went all the way back to the ranch.

Buford and Monarch had a unique relationship, and they also had something in common: both were exhibitionists and loved an audience. As part of his "act," Buford, with a coterie of dudes as an audience, would step into the corral and pet Monarch. The bull would stand docilely while the spectators viewed with awe this demonstration of understanding between man and beast. A bull is a dangerous animal and a potential killer; however, Buford and Monarch seemed to have achieved a state of respectful coexistence.

Monarch was the exact replica of the bull featured in Bull Durham Tobacco advertising. Bull Durham billboards, with a rampant bull prancing across the scene, looked down upon tourists speeding westward on the Lincoln Highway, the nation's very first transcontinental highway. The picture of a cowboy rolling his cigarette, a string bag held between his teeth while building a smoke, stamped the memories of generations who traveled along the highway. Serial Burma-Shave signs, with their simple, silly rhymes, were a counterpoint to the Bull Durham billboards. These artistic ads broke the monotony during long, lonely stretches on the road across the plains.

D. W. Keene

Riding on horseback up a dirt road that led to the foot of the mountains, Buford wanted to check a little valley he believed had been overlooked and, therefore, under grazed. It was a notch almost totally concealed by the mountains, where he hoped to find a good stand of grass to pasture his cows and young calves for several weeks.

On the horizon appeared a large cloud of dust moving down the road toward us. Soon we could see the huge black car that caused the disturbance. As it drew near, we could hear a voice singing *Red River Valley* with great gusto. The car stopped as it drew alongside, and a large man with a ruddy complexion stepped out. "D. W., you old goat!' Buford greeted him. "What brings you up into the Stillwater country?" Without preliminaries the man replied, "You and everyone else in this country know D. W. has gone from a millionaire to bankrupt. I have only the clothes on my back and Big Bessy, the Packard. My creditors did not want her.

"School's out, so I figured now is the time to ride the grub line and visit all of my old friends. I've been up to the Rocking Horse and over to the B. K. Bar. I stayed overnight, and they have taken me in and taken good care of me. All they have is their home-cured beef and potatoes to eat, but I already have lived real royally. Before, I was so busy making money that I never had time for my friends. But now, by Jeffrey, I have lots of time to rekindle old friendships. Don't know why I wasn't smart enough to do it long ago.

"I am telling you, Buford, this is the most fun I have had in years. I am footloose and fancy free. Call the dog and piss on the fire! I have found out where my true values are. They are in my good friends and my associations. By God, Buford, you are among them!"

A large brass-bound trunk and a case of whiskey were the only items in the back seat of the Packard. D. W. reached in and brought forth a big bottle. He took a great swig from the bottle and passed it on to Buford, who did likewise. I, too, took a sip of the Jameson Irish Whiskey. At that, they sat down in a pleasant state of euphoria and talked over old times. Later, as D. W. drove down the road, we could hear the lyrics of *Red River Valley* fading in the distance.

Buford then told me the story. D. W. had come west from Dixon, Illinois, just 18 miles from Mt. Morris, my hometown. For years, D. W. had been the largest Packard dealer between Minneapolis and Seattle. During the good years, he sold so many Packards throughout the Western Dakotas and Montana that he and Packard became synonymous in the region. Packard was the real prestige car of the era, outshining all of its rivals—Cadillac and the rest.

Owning a Packard was an announcement that an individual had become somebody. It gave one an identity. A Packard cost twice as much as General Motors or Ford cars, but it lasted forever. D. W.'s particular model was a twin-six, 12-cylinder car that could run up and down the buttes, over the old cow trails, and across the range. It was big, almost big enough to be a home.

D. W. also had lots of prestige in Detroit, but he was caught in the Great Depression with many delinquent payments, most of which he had financed himself. He was forced to close his agency with a large inventory of unsellable Packards in stock. He went the way many others went during that time, into bankruptcy.

Buford told me that at the peak of his career D. W. owned one of the largest cattle spreads in the Sweetwater country. He did not have to brand his cattle because, at that time, he was the only rancher in that part of the state who ran Black Angus. The rest were all white-faced Herefords. Today Black Angus would undoubtedly outnumber the Herefords.

At any rate, D. W. was a liberated and happy man the day we met him. As a sequel, D. W., aided by affluent friends in Detroit, later made a big comeback as one of the largest dude-ranch operators in the West.

D. W. Keene was typical of some of the giants, bigger than life, who lived on the cutting edge. They rolled the dice and took their chances, adding greatly to the color and the drama of the West.

Line Camp

Occasionally a rancher would acquire a federal grazing lease or purchase a piece of grazing land or hay meadow to extend his holdings. This land would offer temporary grazing and hayfields to support some of his cattle during the season. These tracts were usually quite separate from the main operation. Therefore, they usually included a small cabin located near a spring or tributary, where a part-time cowboy could hole up to perform whatever functions were prescribed by the rancher. These isolated outposts were called line camps.

The cowboys hired to man these isolated outposts were usually older, partially retired riders from the surrounding communities. The line camp custodian was hauled up to the camp with a stock of supplies to last approximately one month. Quantities of beef jerky, beans, flour, and canned vegetables and fruits were his provisions. No doubt his diet was supplemented by fish from adjoining streams or mountain lakes and some illegal hunting. He was left in complete solitude for weeks at a time. He was on his own.

Although it was a solo sojourn for the keeper of the camp, the lonely life lasted for relatively short periods of a month or so between the spring and fall round ups. The line camp custodian had to be resourceful to meet the challenges of his daily routine, which might include building or repairing fences, checking the level of the stock ponds, or maintaining the cattle.

The long-isolated term of a sheepherder was much more dramatic in its effect on the herder. Later, single herdsmanship was frowned upon.

The following story was told in the cow camps, somewhat facetiously, regarding a lone sheepherder: It seems that one early autumn day a cowman was fly fishing a mountain stream when he encountered a large herd of sheep. He spotted the herder, an incongruous figure swaddled in many layers of clothing. His beard was wild and bushy, and his long hair fell to his shoulders. The herder apparently had been isolated with the flock for some time. An altercation ensued, and the cattleman claimed the shepherd became totally incoherent as he grappled with him. In the struggle that followed, the cowman cut away three sets of underwear in which the sheepherder's chest hair had become enmeshed. This apparent act of mercy relieved the sheepherder's discomfort, and he regained his good humor. The two then built a fire and sat down for a bit of grub, coffee, and conversation.

This story is no doubt fiction and probably is more complimentary to the sheepherders than most told by cattlemen of the times. It must be noted that such tales were in vogue not long after the critical cattle vs. sheep wars in Wyoming. The line camp, with all of its testing of the human condition, was far less dramatic than the many tales of the sheepherders that were generated by the cowboys occupying those camps.

During that summer in the Stillwater country, a rumor was current in the valley that a herd of some 8,000 sheep was in desperate circumstances because of the drought. They were being pushed into the Stillwater Valley by Basque herders, sheep men who originated in Spain.

There was very little grass to spare for the home herds. However, Buford had a reserve of several hundred acres of grass on his Trout Creek holding.

In a short time the sheep herd began pouring into the valley. There was little feed for sale at any price, but the herders found out that Buford had some ungrazed grassland. They approached him in their desperation; they had to find feed or lose the flock. Although Buford held most of the same prejudices other cattlemen had against the sheepherders, he did permit them to graze the flock on his land. To ensure that they did not become too enamored of the region, he held up the poor herders for a terrific price.

The Rustler

One day Buford said, "Duke, let's make a trip up to the line camp and check on how old Larry is taking care of the cattle. I know that the salt lick is running low, so we'll take along a few salt blocks for the cattle and some candy for Larry."

We rode for several hours, and as we came towards the camp, Buford pulled up with his hand raised to stop. He said, "Duke, I smell smoke from somewhere up the trail." He paused and said, "Let's proceed slowly."

Before long we detected a thin curl of smoke rising from a clearing. At the same moment, someone on horseback disappeared into the heavy timber that bordered the line camp holding. As we came into the clearing, there was a small fire smoldering with a deep bed of coals—a branding fire. Buford dismounted to read the intruder's tracks. He also examined the smoldering fire closely. I, too could smell burned hair and hide within the fire circle.

We had tied our horses to the ground while Buford squatted to read the trail signs. He finally concluded, "Duke, there is no doubt about it. We've interrupted the work of Bart Mitchell, one of the best rustlers on the range."

Mitchell plied his trade with a finely shaped running iron. He could change any brand in the registry. After changing brands on the cattle, Mitchell and his partner apparently drove them to their secluded hideout, which was believed to be deep in the Hole-in-the-Wall country of Wyoming. Usually, the rightful owners did not discover their losses until late in the fall round up. By then Mitchell and his partner had driven the cattle to a blind market for sale.

Bart Mitchell's string of luck finally ran out, however. He was apprehended and sent to the state prison at Deer Lodge for a long term of incarceration.

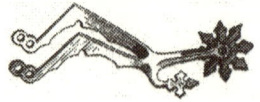

The Gunfighter

Some men are known for that intangible called "presence." Smoke Roberts could qualify for anonymity, both physically and for his very lack of presence. He could fade away unnoticed even in a small group.

He stood perhaps five feet seven and weighed about 135 pounds. He was clean-shaven with features set in a narrow head covered with thick gray hair that had been coal black in his younger years. His eyes were bright blue. He was a neat, diminutive man, quiet with a disarming, almost diffident, manner. He was a gunfighter.

Sam Brown's Hardware was the gathering place for a coterie of survivors who came up with the trail herds from Texas in the 1880s. Sam had cleared out a seating area among the stacks of hand tools; it was heated by an old laundry stove during cold weather. This created a snug haven where the old-timers reminisced about their glory days.

When Buford and I were in Absarokee, we always joined the group at Sam's. Buford was a participant, and I was an interested spectator. Smoke was a silent member.

I learned of Smoke's past from Buford. He had it firsthand from Smoke's old riders who made the long journeys with the herds up the Chisholm and the Goodnight Trails into Montana.

Smoke did not work the cattle. He was always on the edge of the drive, keeping close to the chuck wagon and to the buckaroos in the night camp. He knew the cowboys' foibles and personalities, and their potential for a quarrel. The close association of the men on grueling drives that lasted for months—and traveled at a rate of just several miles a day—created the potential for catastrophe.

Second in command to the trail boss, Smoke was a hired gun for the owners of the big cow brands. He usually settled any personal vendettas with tact or tough action. The riders knew his reputation and feared and respected him. He was the law on the trail northward.

Occasionally, a front rider would find Smoke in privacy throwing stones in the air, drawing his gun and shattering them before they hit the earth. He did not aim; he was a gun pointer of unerring marksmanship.

Smoke was a gunfighter with a record that reached back along the Brazos in Texas. He also had a reputation in the camp towns where grass had been reserved for the herds moving northward. He was rated the fastest gun north of the Red River.

Along the trail there was dubious entertainment for the men. In saloons, the riders could let off pent-up steam with whiskey and women. Abilene, Dodge, North Platte, Shoshoni, and others became landmarks of the journey. Each town had its Boot Hill and its legends, which have become history. Smoke was always nearby when his boys went to town—quiet, alert, and ready to protect his cowpunchers.

A member of one cattle drive told Buford of an incident that took place in a smoky saloon in Abilene: The music stopped. Men and women pushed to the sidelines. There was a burst of profanity from the two adversaries, followed by a hushed silence. In this life-or-death confrontation, Smoke stepped in and shouted, "I'm calling you McVickers!" He drew in a flash and killed his opponent, who took two bullets before he hit the floor. And the music started up again.

Many of the lawmen, gamblers, and outlaws who became part of the legend of the Old West were survivors of the Civil War. Others were spawned by the bands that looted the frontier villages and raided the wagon trains moving westward after the war.

Wild Bill Hickok, Wyatt Earp, and Doc Holliday are part of a litany of famous gunfighters who made their mark on the turbulent cow towns of their day. Hundreds of actors like John Wayne, Gary Cooper, and Clint Eastwood have paraded across the silver screen to burn the images of the gunfighter into the minds and hearts of millions of theatergoers. *High Noon, The Gunfight at O.K. Corral,* and other Hollywood classics are etched in our imaginations. The reading public continues to thrive on Westerns that follow in the style of Owen Wister's first classic, *The Virginian.*

I contend that none of the Western films or novels, all striving to depict the experience of the Old West and its gunfighters, could match the drama, action, and pathos of a real shootout. Those who were there to witness Smoky Roberts draw his weapon experienced something the rest of us will never truly understand.

The Remittance Man

There's a four-pronged buck a-swinging in the shadow of my
cabin
And it roamed the velvet valley till to-day.
But I tracked it by the river, and I trailed it in the cover,
And I killed it on the mountain miles away.

—Robert Service, from "The Rhyme of the Remittance Man"

Clippety-clop, clippety-clop, the remittance man came riding into town as I sat on the porch of the Grand Hotel in Absarokee. The hotel keeper had announced that the remittance man was due for his monthly visit to the post office. We could hear him before we could see him.

As he came into the village, mounted on his hot-blooded thoroughbred, the rhythmic rack turned into the symphony of posting as his mount responded to his horsemanship. As he turned the corner down the main street, I had the impression of a guardsman on parade. He was garbed in an English riding habit: hunting jacket, saddle pants, and highly polished English riding boots with shiny dress spurs.

As he dismounted, he greeted the hotel keeper and handed him the reins. The stableman appeared and led the horse away. He was admonished to rub down and curry the horse and to see that it received an extra ration of oats and fresh, clean bedding. It was clear that the physical condition of the horse was of the utmost importance.

In the meantime, the Englishman was shown to his room, which had been reserved for his monthly visit. He retired to the adjoining bath to remove the dust and dirt from his long journey. He was then ready for a bit of libation, followed by dinner and a rendezvous at the local house of prostitution.

The madam, who knew him well, greeted him warmly while they had a drink in the parlor. They caught up on the news since his last visit. She reviewed for him what her house had to offer, and he soon selected his choice from among the "ladies of the evening." It was late when he returned to his room at the hotel. This monthly interlude filled a gap in the lonely life of the remittance man.

Quite early in the morning, he walked to the post office and collected his monthly check from England. He then went to the general store, where he filled his long list of staples for the coming month. He returned to the hotel, paid his bill, and saw that his horse was fed and groomed before he rode back to the store and filled his saddlebags with his goods.

The sun was well up as his horse hit its stride. Clippety-clop, clippety-clop, and the remittance man returned to the loneliness of his ranch and the challenges of the range.

Late that afternoon, as the sun dropped behind the mountain peaks, the hotel keeper explained to me the history and origin of the remittance man. Back in the corridors of history, there were many warriors who bravely served the British Empire. The king, in turn, bestowed them with titles and large grants of land as reward for their loyalty and valor. They became the landed gentry of England, and their class prospered through the Industrial Revolution.

In England, the eldest son inherited the estate, ensuring the longevity of the family name and dynasty. He would usually help his younger brother(s) and try to arrange affluent marriages for any sisters. With few career choices, younger sons usually went to Sandhurst for careers as army officers or entered the navy as midshipmen following their graduation from Dartmouth. They often entered the Anglican ministry. If none of these careers was acceptable, they were sent to various regions of the empire. These were the remittance men, the younger sons of the titled noblemen of England. They received a monthly stipend, a remittance, from their wealthy families in England. Thus, they were called remittance men. This term has been largely lost in the vocabulary and little has been told about them.

A number of the remittance men were sent to the American West. Some were wastrels and some were intellectuals. Others played an important role in the breeding of American beef cattle and the development of the Western cattle business.

The remittance men imported some of the classic beef breeds such as the white-faced Herefords from England and the Black Angus from Scotland. These animals replaced the lean, long-legged longhorns that originated from the early Spanish and Texas ranches. These imported breeds had a square confirmation with short legs and carried plenty of quality beef.

Some of the remittance men became associated with the largest cattle outfits of the West. The sons of many settled and remained in America. Their history and achievements have largely faded into the history of the West.

Buying the Dunbar Ranch

My Montana interlude was drawing to a close. It had packed the action and history of years into one sweet summer of youth.

Furthermore, I had an important date coming up, a wedding to marry the girl back home. Margaret, my eventual wife of 70 years, and I had solemnly agreed that my summer in the West would provide an interval for contemplation, as well as a test of our intention to become lifetime partners. Such is the romantic stuff of youth. I had written her that as far as I was concerned, the test was fulfilled, and I hoped that our wedding would occur shortly after my return. She concurred. This would be a high point of the summer.

In the meantime, life was beginning to heat up in my area of Montana. For several weeks, one of the main topics of conversation up and down the Stillwater was the forthcoming auction of the Dunbar Ranch.

During the drought and depression of the thirties, there were many ranch sales. Range land was selling for two to five dollars an acre; irrigated meadow brought twenty to thirty dollars. The selling was slow because few prospective buyers had any money.

The Dunbar Lazy D was almost at the end of the road approaching the foot of the Beartooth Range. It was highly regarded as one of the gems on a string of jewels along the river running up to the foot of the Beartooth Mountains. It formed a basin with the Stillwater River flowing through the center. The formation encompassed 160 acres of alfalfa fields that straddled the river. The entire plot was "under the ditch," with its own water supplying the meadow from the irrigation canal that circled the top edge of the basin.

Of the long chain of ranches along the Stillwater River, the Lazy D had third call on the water. The river was an unfailing source for irrigation in the valley.

A 1,600-acre government lease on the nearby public domain was part of the title to be conveyed at the time of the sale. Grazing rights were twenty-five cents per head per year. It was an excellent summer range and mountain meadow with a good stand of grass backed up by those 160 acres of hay for wintering the herd. This lease, which came with the title, was a valuable asset to the Dunbar Ranch.

Snowcapped peaks stood up in the background with waterfalls dropping down the sides in sheets of silver that appeared stationary from the distance. Just over the range lay Yellowstone Park. The ranch—with the priceless asset of water—was as self-sufficient as any in this precarious country and as beautiful as a picture postcard.

The only building left on the home site was the old blacksmith shop. The others had been burned to the ground, either by prospectors who had come years before, or as a result of a lightning strike.

At the time of the auction, Dink Masterson had eighty head of four- and five-year-old steers grazing on the ranch land. He had been holding them on cheap rent waiting for a better market. Everyone expected Masterson to buy the ranch. He was using it already, and people presumed he was one of the few people in the area who had some money.

The auctioneer was chanting, but the bidding was very slow. Dink had bid $1,200, and the auctioneer was pleading for some competition. He extolled the obvious merits of the ranch, exhorting his audience to buy the bargain of a lifetime. This was more truthful than even he imagined. But the crowd was mostly there for a social event. They had barely survived the long drought and years of depression; they had no funds to bid. It was apparent that the sale was reaching the final stages, and the auctioneer was hanging on the last bid.

Buford, who was a nervous man when excited, started jumping up and down, tugging at my shoulders. "Duke, do you have any money? This is one of the best ranches in Stillwater country. Don't let anyone steal it. This country has to come up. It's as flat on its back as it can get."

I was startled. I longed for land, but it never occurred to me to buy land in this far, dry country. I told him I had saved $1,200, but I was getting married as soon as I got back home.

Buford continued to shout. People were looking and listening. "Never mind that. Buy this ranch!"

From somewhere in the crowd came a bid of $1,300. Under the spell of Buford's intense persuasion, I heard myself shouting, "$1,400!" and then the auctioneer chanting, "Going, going, gone." I had bought the Dunbar Ranch—lock, stock, and barrel.

The lawyer seemed quite skeptical when I told him the money would come from Illinois. He assured me that unless I settled within 20 days, I would have to pay all expenses for this and another sale. Rather miraculously, $1,200 did arrive from my home bank in short time. This was held in forfeit for the balance, which I borrowed with the ranch as collateral. I had become another financially strapped ranch owner.

An aftermath of the sale was Buford's fear that Dink Masterson might become violent when asked to surrender the ranch. Dink was one of the trail herders who came up the Chisholm to Montana. He was a Texan whose family had migrated to Texas after the fall of the Confederacy. Some said there was a colony of these Southerners who continued to rule that area under the flag of the Stars and Bars for a number of years. They were fighters and violent men, and Dink Masterson was considered to be one of that breed.

So one morning I saddled up one of Buford's trail horses and headed for my destiny at the Dunbar Ranch. The horse kept stride with a good running walk. My fear of a confrontation with that old trail driver haunted me on that ride. In the past, possession was considered nine-tenths of the law. Buford's fear of trouble made me increasingly uneasy as I approached the Dunbar. I knew Dink Masterson would be there for the final cutting of the hay crop. I neck-reined my horse through the gateway with a feeling of fear and curiosity. I pulled to a stop as Dink came towards me. There was something menacing in his appearance that could have been taken from the O.K. Corral. As he stood beside my offside stirrup, he said with a soft Southern accent. "Step down from your horse. I know who you are, and I've got a pot boiling on the fire. I really wanted this ranch, but time is running out for me. I have no heirs. I'm reconciled to your purchase, and I feel the Dunbar will be in good hands."

After our meal, I learned about the life and times of Dink Masterson. He had been a trail rider with several herds traveling up from the Brazos and different points in Texas. He had saved enough to pay for his own ranch, which was over on Little-Big-Woman Creek, a tributary of the Stillwater. His holdings were much larger than the Dunbar, but he was using the grass and meadow to sustain his old, heavy steers. They were worth about a nickel a pound, and he was hoping for a better market in St. Paul.

Each fall the ranchers shipped a number of carloads of cattle on the Burlington Railroad to the St. Paul market. Some of them accepted a free ticket for the round trip to St. Paul and back in the caboose. During the good years, this trip was a festive occasion for the cowmen, the topic of conversation for the long winter months.

Dink and I parted good friends. He moved his cattle from the ranch and was able to sell them in a bit stronger market. He is among my most pleasant memories in the saga of the Dunbar Ranch.

After buying the ranch, I began to wrestle with the stark realization that I had no money to start wedded life. I didn't even have enough to finance the honeymoon. My mind was so heavy with doubt and misgivings that I wondered how I could have been so rash. The ranch was 1,400 miles away from the lush, civilized country of Illinois.

Mercifully, Buford stepped in and reassured me, and the optimism of youth prevailed. Buford said I should return to my good job, get married, and work for three years, gathering a stake to stock the ranch. Then I should return with my bride and start ranching. In the meantime, he would build a good log house, a corral, and a small barn on the ranch. He would do this in exchange for three years' rent on the land. He had done all of this and more on his ranch so I knew he was competent; it could be a good deal for both of us. I told him I would give him my final answer after discussing the plan thoroughly with Margaret. I continued to dream and to ponder what the future might bring.

Back to Illinois

It was late summer and I was going home, back to Illinois. I had spent the night on the Wind River, and all that morning, the image of the snowcapped Wind River Range was in my rear view mirror.

Later in the day, I stopped at a log inn lost in the vast stretches of Wyoming. There were two other travelers there. The supper the innkeeper served was surprisingly good.

One of my table companions was a slender, well-dressed man, probably in his forties. His smartly tailored coat covered a contrasting vest, and a black string tie with long ends completed his natty appearance. He was not handsome, but his features were even and pleasant, giving him a look of intelligence. He was soft-spoken and conveyed the impression of courteous reserve. It was evident that he was literate and well educated.

The autumn chill of the country had settled on the land. The cheery flames of the fireplace cast shadows that danced on the walls. Over a drink from the adjacent bar, the warm glow permeated the room. It was an ideal setting for the kind of revealing conversation that comes only with the spontaneity of passing travelers.

The fortunes of the road had brought us together, and as we filled the time with conversation, it was apparent that my new acquaintance was knowledgeable on a wide range of topics. Beneath, there was a quiet reserve of a gentleman who held at arm's length any information of a personal nature. We discussed a multitude of subjects before I realized he had divulged very little about himself.

We were about to turn in when he casually mentioned that we were both going east in the morning. He added that his car had thrown a connecting rod and would be in the shop for two weeks before parts would be available from the East. His car was a Jordan Playboy, broken down on its way east. It was ironic that the car-maker's recent ad campaign touted, "Somewhere in Wyoming there's a Jordan Playboy coursing westward." He paused slightly before he said, "We seem to fill in the time quite well. In the event you would care to continue, I would be glad to ride with you in the morning. I'm traveling eastward on some business. At any rate, I have no problem either way, and we will part good friends. Let's see how it looks in the morning. Good night!"

When I came down to breakfast, the host said my friend had been there before me and mentioned he would be in his room. He had left the choice to me. I tapped on his door. When he appeared, I asked him if he was ready to travel. He responded by closing his bag and saying he was all clear.

It was a beautiful morning, and we had been on the road for about two hours when something happened that struck me with a sudden uneasiness bordering on fear. I had an ominous feeling that despite our pleasant evening, I really knew nothing about this well-mannered man turned out in expensive tailoring.

This was a vast country. Anything could happen in the long stretches of fifty to a hundred miles between towns, and probably no one would ever know what happened. The cause of my uneasiness occurred when he reached across to pull out the ashtray. As he did so, the front of his coat fell open. I had a clear look at a shoulder holster, complete with revolver, under his left armpit. He noticed at once that I had seen the gun. With a quizzical smile he assured me that I had no reason for alarm.

Many travelers in the West carried guns in their cars, but it was apparent that he preferred to keep his where it would be most convenient. He saw that it was now necessary to reveal some answers to my unasked questions. Consequently, I learned that he was a professional gambler. He plied his trade throughout the West, including the length of California. He had worked as a faro dealer in San Francisco and other cities. Currently, he was working a scheduled poker circuit that started in Montana, carried on into Wyoming, and continued into Western Nebraska. The next game was set for the town where we expected to spend the night.

He explained that the gun was a precaution to be used only if a tense situation arose during a game. However, it was mostly carried as protection against being relieved of his stake when returning to his hotel late at night.

During the course of our ride, he revealed enough of his career to form a partial profile of the man who had become my travel partner. Apparently, he came from a solid merchant family in England. The gambler had migrated to Virginia and drifted into the gambling fraternity that plied its trade on inland riverboats. He was not a remittance man. He stood entirely on his own resources.

I asked him if he had ever gambled in Illinois. He replied that he had once made a three-day stand at the Elks' picnic in LaSalle, Illinois. I told him that was only sixty miles from my hometown.

Apparently the Elks were having a big annual affair, and part of the midway housed a faro game. However, by that time faro dealers were scarce, and most had become a part of history. He saw an ad in the *Police Gazette* stating that the Elks were seeking a faro dealer for three days at the LaSalle convocation. They offered to pay expenses and $100 a day for a professional faro dealer. He applied and immediately got the job. That was the only occasion when he returned back east of the Mississippi.

Late in the day we came into Gordon, Nebraska, parked the car at the hotel, and registered for the night. With a straight look into each other's eyes, we shook hands, and he thanked me for my courtesies before he went up to his room. I never saw him again.

Several days later, I rolled into Mt. Morris, my Western adventures at an end. The wedding came off as planned, and it was the highlight of my summer. I did, however, have to borrow money for my honeymoon.

Although Margaret at first had some trouble understanding the expenditure of my entire fortune on a ranch 1,400 miles away, she became resolved to the fact. Our parents were less enthusiastic with my new acquisition, especially after the plight of the West made the front page news—the drought, the grasshoppers, and people leaving Montana in droves. My father said, "You should buy land, but not Montana land. It won't support a crow flying over it. The only good land is Illinois or Iowa land."

I had intended to take my bride back to the ranch and to accept Buford's offer to build us a strong house in exchange for rent on the land. Unfortunately, my plan seemed to be unraveling rapidly. I was very discouraged at that point.

Shortly thereafter a telegram arrived from a Billings lawyer offering to purchase the Dunbar Lazy D Ranch for $1,800, providing me with a $400 profit on the entire deal. I thought it was fate and quickly accepted the offer.

Many years later, Margaret and I returned to the Dunbar Ranch. The owner was the same man who had bought it from me long ago. He said, "I have been offered $400,000 cash for the Dunbar, and that is more than it's worth, but I know what I want and I got it."

Through most of my life, a man's worth was measured by his tangible assets: land, cattle, gold, silver. These were the solid, long-term holdings that could be built into a family dynasty, and for thousands of years such property was the measurement of a man's wealth. Today, wealth is evaluated by paper securities and floating prophesies of the future. I never gave up on land as a valued commodity. I've always been intrigued by real estate, which my father said was not transient property vulnerable to the whimsies of speculators and stockbrokers.

During my lifetime, I have owned real estate in Minnesota's Red River Valley, Montana, Colorado, at the foot of the Sangre de Cristo Mountains, and, best of all, in Northwestern Illinois. My River Hill farm lies between the Rock and Mississippi Rivers in the Northwestern corner of Illinois. The native grass is green and lush; hardwood trees cast their shadows along the back roads of this beautiful country. The hills break away from the prairie into upland, where farms can carry a cow and a calf to an acre. In contrast, Montana is, and was, a young man's country, subject to violent episodes of drought and severe seasonal change—a country of feast or famine.

However, my interlude in Montana remains engraved in my memory through the years. I continue to remember that summer long ago, and those recurring dreams of the West still descend upon me as the dawn breaks. That golden time spent in the summer of

1931 is a treasured episode of a life that has spanned nearly a century.

Epilogue

My story would not be complete without a sequel to the life and times of Buford and Hazel Kratz.

The fortunes of the Reverse ⅍ Bar Ranch grew with the national economy. Buford and Hazel added some native help to take care of the business at the ranch.

Buford, a pioneer booster, saw his prophecies coming true. He started the only real estate agency in Stillwater country. As a skillful raconteur, he could eloquently relate the history and the romance of the West. This intrigued his clientele as well as many newcomers to the area who sought him out. After some years of living on the edge as the proprietor of a struggling dude and cattle ranch, his fortunes began to expand beyond his wildest dreams. He began selling real estate to Hollywood celebrities and professionals from the East.

By then, Buford had acquired several miles of riverfront property along the Stillwater. As demand for Montana river property increased and it soared in value, he decided that his property had become too valuable to keep. He sold it at prices far beyond his expectations. His real estate agency boomed and dominated the center of the little cow town of Absarokee. His huge sign on the main street was the first to meet the eye of the stranger entering the town.

Buford knew that the West was the country of boom and bust, constantly threatened by the gods of weather and the national economy. Empowered by the momentum of the boom, his business expanded into a widening periphery reaching beyond Columbus and Big Timber, and on into the territories surrounding Absarokee.

Hazel and Buford's lifestyle took on some of the trappings of the *nouveau riche.* Hazel worked in the office while Buford was in the field selling Montana, generally, and the river, specifically.

Hazel wore expensive tailored suits purchased in an exclusive shop in Billings. Obviously, this was a big change from her ranch attire. Her carefully coiffed hair and immaculate appearance added a professional touch to the agency.

Buford was attired in his best Levis and a cowboy shirt, topped off by an expensive Stetson. He was shod in fine Justin boots. As a finishing touch, he adorned his left hand with a full-carat diamond ring.

Betty June on Sox

Hazel and Buford had one daughter, Betty June. She was a good-looking girl with her mother's fine features and reserved refinement of speech. She was the first of the family to graduate from the University of Montana. Later, she married a young lawyer. He set up a law office in Absarokee and became a partner in the Kratz realty firm, hastening his climb up the ladder of success. Later, he moved Betty June to a country house near Salisbury, England. The house featured a skylight view of the cathedral spire once depicted by the famous artist, Arnold Constable. Betty June, the mother of four children, became a pure Anglophile in this environment.

On at least one occasion, she persuaded her mother and father to fly to England for a prolonged visit. There might have been some question as to whether Buford, with his Western mannerisms, would be fully accepted in English society.

Buford arrived in England dressed in his opulent cattle rancher's garb: diamond ring, Stetson hat, Justin boots, the full works. Needless to say, this was a far cry from the well-known British style of understatement, but the British loved it! Buford lived up to their colorful picture of a cowboy from the American West. He was literally placed on exhibition in his daughter's social circles.

After some years Betty June returned to America and divorced her husband. Her children graduated from British schools and remained in England. She now lives in Absarokee and makes periodic trips to England to visit her family.

Buford and Hazel, after selling their ranch on the Stillwater, enjoyed the luxuries that their long-time faith in Montana and its rivers produced. Buford built one of the finest homes in the village of Absarokee. They lived in it for several years, until an *outsider* moved into town and built an even more pretentious home. Buford could not overlook this intruder. He built yet another home, even more ostentatious than either his first home or that of the interloper. To cap off his success, Buford bought a new Cadillac every other year. He had truly achieved the American Dream.

Hazel participated in the rise to success in her reserved manner. She was not the colorful exhibitionist that her husband was.

As the couple grew older, they joined the ranks of the early commercial air travelers. They usually spent winter in a warmer climate.

One of their interesting travel adventures occurred when a group of Montana cattlemen from the pioneer ranch families of the state chartered a train to the World's Fair in New York. This was an extravaganza that required considerable capital and imagination. The train consisted of a section of sleeping cars, observation decks, a full-course dining car, and last but not least, a number of well-equipped stock haulers for their horses and equipment.

Stops were scheduled at various cities and towns across the continent. Buford invited my friend, Elmer Paul, and me to Moline, Illinois, where they would make a scheduled stop. Elmer and I, with our wives, Annis and Margaret, were waiting when the train arrived. The engineer gave a lingering blast of the horn and braked the train to a halt. Instantly, entire sections of the train came alive with ranchers dressed in their best regalia unloading their saddle horses.

Horses and riders moved into parade formation. The band played *Red River Valley* as they paraded down the streets of Moline. They were the pride and legend of Montana—the long, lean line of men and women who represented the West. They even made the front page in newspapers across the continent.

We had a catch-up lunch with Buford and Hazel while the horses were being reloaded for the journey. The Moline stop provided a wonderful opportunity for us to renew our friendship and to glean the news of their current lives.

As the Montana contingent arrived in New York, they were hailed and cheered by people from all parts of the world. They represented the grandeur, the drama, and the legend of the American cowboy that had stepped out of the literature and legend of the West. They were on their last great round up.

An auto collision crippled Hazel in the following years. She later suffered from Alzheimer's disease, which marked the end of their traveling days. Buford and Betty June took care of Hazel for several years until she passed on prior to Buford.

Buford lived to the age of eighty. His mortal remains were placed on a work wagon hitched to a lively team of horses and pulled to the cemetery overlooking the river—and the ranch land he knew and loved so dearly.

The branding fire is burning low,
the night rider is singing his song,
and the last of the Conestoga wagons
are at rest by the wayside.
A galleon moon is coming up over
the Beartooth, illuminating the sea of grass
that sustained the trail herds
on their long journey to Montana.
All seems well as this writer
heads toward the Final Roundup.
"O, bury me-e-e-e on the lone prairie-e-e-e,
and let the coyotes howl over me."

About the Author

Clarence Mitchell's career as a printer started during the hand-set days and carried right through to the hot-lead composition of the Monotype and Linotype machines. His name was on the door as Editorial Director of Production at Kable Printing Company (now Quebecor World, Inc.), one of the nation's largest printers. He also did considerable ghostwriting while in this position.

He retired at sixty. Mitchell and Margaret, his wife of nearly seventy years, traveled extensively and at various times lived in England. He hoped to pay his way as a free-lance writer (and sometimes he did).

He is a supporter of higher education and was a charter member of the Board of Trustees of Highland Community College in Freeport, Illinois. The Mitchell Library is on the Highland Campus. He is also a backer of Manchester College in Indiana, a Church of the Brethren school.

As a journalist, he is a patron of WHA, the public television station at the University of Wisconsin at Madison.

Before embarking on this book, Mitchell completed two others: *River Hill Soliloquy* and *The Diary of a Journeyman*. The first captures his long-time love affair with his farm, which is situated in his favorite slice of America, Northwestern Illinois. The second is a recording of many of his recollections of those he met, the places he visited, and the events he experienced over ninety-seven years.

Approaching his centennial year, and with the encouragement of friends, Mitchell was persuaded to write *Montana Montage*, which chronicles his summer of 1931 on a dude ranch in Montana and illustrates a slice of the transition from the Old West to the West of today. Mitchell remains a romanticist and believes the profession is ever riding down to Camelot. This book lends credence to his claim.

He continues to live in his home in Mt. Morris, Illinois. From there, he sallies forth into the hinterlands to enjoy his many associates and the beauties of that part of the world. He never tires of looking for new roads to travel and new adventures to add to his memories.

Clarence Mitchell, Montana, 1930s

978-0-595-37845-6
0-595-37845-5

www.ingramcontent.com/pod-product-compliance
Lightning Source LLC
Chambersburg PA
CBHW030342290526
45785CB00004B/1566